Open Hearts and Open Doors

Radical Hospitality in the UU Church

Kenneth P. Langer

Brass Bell Books

BRASS BELL
BOOKS & GAMES

Contents

Introduction

The Vision

I n 1989, the Unitarian Universalist Association's (UUA) Common Vision Planning Committee issued a document entitled "Proposals of the Common Vision." That plan included recommendations for the UUA and its member congregations on how to begin the work of inviting and accepting LGBTQ and other gender fluid people into the folds of UU congregational life. The result of those proposals led to the Welcoming Congregations Program whose stated goal was to ensure that, "lesbian, gay, bisexual, transgender, and queer people are full members of our faith communities." As a result of those efforts, the website proclaims, a large majority of UU congregations are designated as "Welcoming Congregations."

In 2020, the UUA issued a report entitled "Widening the Circle of Concern" in response to ongoing acts of racial injustice throughout the United States. The group was "charged with supporting long-term cultural and institutional change that redeems the essential promise and ideals of Unitarian Universalism." One section of the report focused on hospitality and inclusion. Its introduction states that, "though our predominantly white congregations and organizations may see themselves as welcoming, without particular practices, they continue to mirror the kinds of harms done to people of color and other marginalized groups in our larger society."

In 2022, the UUA issued a Statement of Conscience entitled "Undoing Systemic White Supremacy: A Call To Prophetic

Action" with the stated goal of making "our congregations and communities authentically multicultural, multiracial, anti-oppressive spaces that dismantle anti-Blackness." The intention was to build relationships across perceived boundaries between BIPOC (black, indigenous, and people of color) individuals and predominantly white UU congregations.

What all these efforts call for is radical inclusion that goes beyond just inviting particular groups of people into congregational life. In Unitarian Universalism there is now a conscious effort to fully embrace and welcome all people regardless of sexual identity, racial background, economic status, or any other factors.

One way to achieve the goals of these efforts is through the practice of Radical Hospitality.

Radical Hospitality goes beyond inviting and including people who may be gender fluid into the congregation and expands the mission into doing the same work with the same dedication toward all people. Radical Hospitality is not only an acceptance of others but is a recognition that all people deserve full inclusion into all aspects of UU congregational life in a way that fully values the newcomer.

Why I Started This Project

During the pandemic I became a Unitarian Universalist seminary student. After the first few years of my study and as the pandemic began to wane I started giving sermons throughout New England. I got to observe a lot of UU churches and I became fascinated with how visitors were treated and how they found (or did not find) what they were seeking.

As I entered each church I asked myself what it would be like to be a first time visitor to that church. What would be my first impression? How easy would it be to find my way around? What if I knew nothing about the church or about Unitarian Universalism? Would I be able to understand what I experienced? Would I want to come back? Would my experience have been any different if I was someone traditionally marginalized or oppressed?

Without exception, every church I visited had the basics of hospitality woven into the practices of their congregation. The message that everyone was welcome was printed on bulletins and pamphlets, was sometimes seen on the building itself, and was preached from the pulpit, but the actuality of how people experienced their visit sometimes told a different story. It was often as if visitors were expected to just know or figure out for themselves where to go, who to talk to, what to do, or even what to understand about the theology and mission of the church. People who did decide to return for subsequent visits would first have to contend with a variety of practices and habits of tradition in order to become more involved with the church.

I wanted to find ways in which UU churches could truly become the church that receives, uplifts, and embraces all people in a manner that promotes growth and renewal for everyone involved–newcomer and long-time members alike. What I discovered were some best practices for becoming a truly welcoming and accepting church. I have bundled these practices together under the single name of Radical Hospitality.

I do not claim to be an expert in this area. It has been an area of interest to me because I believe that our movement is important and I believe that there are others who would be a part of it if they knew about it.

When I told people in the churches I visited about my passion for this topic they asked me to share my work with them. This book is my way of sharing what I have learned with others.

My hope in writing this book is to help others find ways to make their churches become microcosms of the great world in which we hope to live. If we want to exist in a world of peace and compassion for all then we can begin by modeling that world through our congregations. Radical Hospitality can be a way to express and demonstrate openness through counter-oppressive behaviors reflected in our actions as well as our facilities.

This project is a work in progress. It is my hope that this will be the beginning of a continuous conversation the results of which will be reflected in future editions of this and other works. I welcome the experiences and practices of others who take on this work to shape and develop it for the betterment of all.

Radical Hospitality

The practices of Radical Hospitality are things the congregation and its Welcoming/Hospitality team can do to make a church more open and supportive for all people. Some ideas are focused on the physical structures of the church and its surrounding grounds. I call these practices Essential Invitation. They are designed to make a church feel like a spiritual home and refuge for all members and seekers alike regardless of identity or background.

Other ideas are centered on the approach and philosophy used when welcoming others to the congregation. These practices are called Radical Welcoming. Radical Welcoming is a movement that encourages churches to become more open to all people but especially to those who have been oppressed by traditions of white supremacy and religious intolerance. Radical Welcoming is accomplished by recognizing that visitors are not strangers but individuals of value and significance each of whom enter the church with unique and important stories and experiences of their own.

Radical Hospitality is the term used here to combine the philosophy of Radical Welcoming with the practices of Essential Invitation.

Radical Hospitality, then, is both an attitude and an environment that accepts and encourages all people to become engaged with the mission, fellowship, and spiritual goals of the church. All actions taken through the process of Essential Invitation are combined with an attitude of Radical Welcoming so that all people involved–both members and newcomers–are honored and supported.

Unitarian Universalism offers a message of hope and compassion for the world. The world we live in includes a multitude of beautiful and diverse people who hold a myriad of religious and philosophical worldviews. The only way that peace can be implemented in such a complex world is to focus on the sanctity of the seeker rather than what is being sought. Unitarian Universalism does not demand adherence to one creed or to one way of doing things. It embraces all theological viewpoints and people of all identities who agree to live in love rather than hate. Radical Hospitality is a way to let others know about our message of compassion and inclusivity and to invite ourselves and others to transform each other into the universal Beloved Community we seek to become.

The Chapters

Chapter One more fully explains the concept of Radical Hospitality and its constituents: Radical Welcoming and Essential Invitation. Chapter Two discusses why Radical Hospitality is an essential part of any church's mission. Unitarian Universalist theology is related to the purposes of Radical Hospitality. The following four chapters are based on the four parts of a complete Radical Hospitality program which are Vision (Chapter Three), Invitation (Chapter Four), Inclusion (Chapter Five), and Transformation (Chapter Six). Vision is the process of defining the purpose and goals of Radical Hospitality while Invitation is the implementation of the goals defined in the Vision. The process of Inclusion works to make sure that the church continues to be inclusive and inviting to everyone while Transformation is an open invitation to the church and all its members to grow and be renewed through interaction with every new and existing member.

Chapter One: Coming To Terms

H ow would you react if you found out that a very special guest was about to come to visit you? Would you make special preparations? Would you spend extra time cleaning? Would you prepare a special meal? Would you put on fancy clothes?

How would you react if a complete stranger suddenly came to visit you? Would you be cautious and defensive? Would you be hesitant to let that person in? Would you be frightened?

The word "stranger" simply means someone with whom you are unfamiliar but words carry connotations developed over many years of use. The word "stranger" often denotes a sense of risk or threat. Children are taught about "stranger danger" so that they avoid being taken advantage of by predators. Movies about The Stranger often depict the unknown character as a unusual and elusive person possibly with bad intentions. The Stranger is an outsider.

The Outsider

Becoming a radically hospitable church challenges us to welcome the outsider with the same intention and enthusiasm as we might the honored guest. The outsider has been someone who looks, acts, or thinks differently than what was traditionally defined as the standard for the dominant culture. The outsider was someone who was excluded from systems of power and opportunity.

This practice of exclusion of the outsider leads to a sense

of shame and guilt for those left out. It creates a false sense of separation that causes suffering for everyone–not just the outsider. Exclusion sends a message to the outsider that they are not worthy of acceptance or recognition and the emotional pain experienced is as real as any physical pain. People who are rejected in one place will seek out another where they can feel accepted.

We are social creatures and being accepted and nurtured within groups is important to all human growth and well-being. Group interaction and cooperation is how humanity learned to survive. This social cohesion is the basis of every spiritual community.

Fear of the outsider has become a way to project anxieties and stress onto people with perceived differences. It is this perception of difference that creates a separation between the insider and the person labeled as the outsider. Too often those differences are influenced more by fear than by biology. Insecurity about economics or social change makes some look for an easy identifiable characteristic or behavior to secure blame.

Who is the outsider, anyway? Every person is unique and different. If people are to be afraid of anyone who appears to be different then we should all be afraid of every single person we meet. What is the true essence of a person? Is it a skin color, hair length, body size, a speech pattern, a particular ability, or is it the values and virtues that remain hidden beyond those physical attributes?

No one can be known simply through visual cues. Who we really are is based on our understanding of our place in this world and how we wish to act within it. Understanding this for our own selves can sometimes take a lifetime. We are barely able to know ourselves within the short period of time we exist on this planet. How is it possible to come to know someone else in the flash of a moment?

In reality, the Stranger is everyone and the Stranger is ourselves. In the span of an entire lifetime we come to learn about our own minds, hearts, and bodies and through the constant process of growth and development we continuously learn and discover. It is through the interaction between people–all strangers–that we learn more about ourselves. Encountering different people is how we grow.

The history of humans has always been tribal in nature. We banded together with other humans in order to hunt and to defend ourselves from other creatures. We looked for signs that told us who was in the tribe and who was not. Though those instincts may run deep in our human development we have also come to develop a mind that is capable of overcoming those fears. Modern society need no longer be tribal. The world is now one tribe of living beings on one unique planet. Our ability to connect and have compassion for each other must become the new pattern for this planet and its children to survive and thrive together. Any other pattern of living into the future will only lead to our own destruction.

The Stranger, then, is everyone, for we can never truly and completely know another. But, we must also realize that we never fully and completely come to know our own selves which makes us the Stranger as much as anyone else. When we stop and pay attention to our own bodies, our own thoughts, and our own feelings; when we take the time to tell our own stories, we develop a better understanding of our own selves. When we pay attention to another person and listen to their stories we develop a better understanding of that person and ourselves.

The Outsider is not a person. The Outsider is the fear we encounter when we are challenged to grow. We fear a change of identity whether it is how we identify ourselves, our community, or our culture but change is the only path to growth and renewal and the only way to defy stagnation and decay.

To be a radically hospitable congregation requires that we wrestle with the fear that comes with change and growth. Not dealing with the fear will result in an attempt to ignore or dismiss it. It is like trying to sweep it under the proverbial rug except that fear is not inert; it is a living thing and when pushed into the dark will only grow and manifest itself into something worse. Dealing with fear requires that we root it out and expose it to the open air.

Without that exposure, fear can be hidden behind a need to hang on to tradition, or an effort to slow down or ignore anything that is novel, or to a claim that there are no resources available.

The way to encounter and overcome fear is not to let it crawl into a dark space. Fear needs to be named and seen. It needs to be given the room and space to settle and be examined in the light. Fear can be softened with compassion and through sharing that compassion with and between each other. Individual and group spiritual practices can be beneficial as can open discussions in safe spaces. Individual and group spiritual practices can be helpful—especially those that can open the mind to curiosity rather than judgment and can open the heart to acceptance rather than rejection.

Who Is Welcome

Radical Hospitality happens when we open our minds, our hearts, and our sacred spaces to those who have been historically oppressed and ignored. This includes not just the LGBTQ and gender fluid communities but also those of all ages, backgrounds, socioeconomic factors, races, abilities, or religious traditions. Furthermore, Radical Hospitality involves a willingness to open our house and receive those who need compassion and care in times of need. These can include but are not limited to circumstances such as when a person's life is threatened or when a person's welfare is endangered. Sometimes we can be a safe haven for those who are in transition such as people escaping abuse or persecution.

The world is no longer an enormous patchwork of unique lands inhabited by unique people. In practical terms, the world is shrinking. Solid borders are melting away as instantaneous interactions across the globe are now possible. We are transforming from lands filled with castles, walls, and guard towers into a global village. Such a change can be slow and painful but it is inevitable and there is no turning back. We either can accept this reality and work to develop a human family on earth or we can continue to fight and reject each other for whatever trivial reasons we may conjure as excuses.

Radical Hospitality begins by accepting the premise that we are all different and yet we are all the same. It acknowledges the fear that comes with any change or transformation and makes room to share and explore that fear. It is a demonstration of the sacred act of welcoming The Stranger beyond us and within us.

Who Is Not Welcome

Though Unitarian Universalists like to say often in both written and spoken words that everyone is welcome the truth is that everyone is not welcome nor should they be. If radical hospitality is an offering of compassion into a congregation that wishes to be a Beloved Community then those who seek to disrupt or destroy that mission are not welcome to be part of it. Those who espouse or condone hatred or violence against others are not welcome.

There are UUs who embrace the practice of non-violence in all situations but there are also those who believe that violence may sometimes be necessary in times of defense or in the fight against injustice. That is not the type of violence being mentioned here. It is hatred or violence meant specifically to oppress, humiliate, shame, or degrade others. This brand of hatred works directly against the principles of Radical Hospitality and the open and welcome church.

Note that this characteristic is not something that somebody IS but is something that somebody DOES. There are no physical traits that determine a degree of hatred or a proclivity for violence; only physical actions reveal those things. A person who wants to enter a church with a loaded gun is not welcome. A person who wears a shirt with a racist logo or phrase is not welcome. Radical Hospitality must include a sense of safety and security for all.

Welcoming and Radical Welcoming

The term Radical Welcoming is meant to be distinguished from just welcoming. The difference may be compared to the contrast between knitting and quilting. In knitting, similar strands of material are knotted together to create an item such as a hat or a scarf. Though there may be a pattern to the design and some changes in color or yarn, the final product is often homogenous and symmetrical in design. When quilting, unique and separate patterns are pieced together. Each individual quilt square adds a uniqueness to the whole design. Lines and colors are not made to form a pattern together. Instead, each square adds a uniqueness to the entire product.

Welcoming is similar to knitting. Different people may be brought into the church but they are asked to weave themselves together into existing systems and patterns. Radical welcoming is more like quilting. It brings people in but makes time to learn about and celebrate the uniqueness that each new person brings with them. The talents and gifts each person offers to the church are displayed proudly and are joined together with the beauty of the diversity that others bring and share. This does not mean that radical welcoming discards tradition and custom. There must always be a strong thread that runs throughout the quilt and holds the pieces together. In UU churches that thread is our principles and covenants.

What Does It Mean To Welcome?

Strictly speaking, the word 'welcome' means to greet someone. The word is derived from an old English term which refers to the presence of someone who is pleasing. This understanding of the word does not tell us what kind of person is welcomed, only that meeting the person should be a pleasurable act. If every encounter with a new person is met with fear there can never be any pleasure in it. The pleasure in meeting someone new, regardless of who that person may be, is that you will learn something novel about that other person, the world, and yourself. Releasing fear and being open to the joy of welcoming others is the first step toward radical welcoming.

What Radical Hospitality Is

The origin of the word 'radical' comes from the word 'root.' It has a connection to the word 'radial' or 'radius.' To be radical is to get to the root or heart of a matter. The Oxford Dictionary explains that radical means to relate or affect the fundamental nature of something.

The fundamental nature of welcoming is to honor and celebrate the uniqueness of each individual who is also very similar to each of us. We are all individually distinctive yet we are all human and humans need each other. When we share our strengths we make ourselves stronger together.

Radical Hospitality, however, goes beyond just welcoming. Radical Hospitality expands welcoming through the idea that fully including the gifts and presence of new people into any organization will transform that organization. A welcoming congregation opens the door to The Outsider while Radical Hospitality congregations open their arms and their hearts to the Outsider. Radical Hospitality must be done with intent and with anticipation of the growth and renewal that will occur with every new encounter.

Radical Hospitality, as the term is used in this book, combines two different aspects of the process of welcoming: Invitation and Inclusion. Invitation is a way of seeing the space so that it can become more appealing and materially welcoming to all people. Inclusion is the philosophy and vision that guides both the welcoming process and the creation of a transformed body of people that results from it. The combination of Invitation and Inclusion is Radical Hospitality.

The difference between hospitality and radical hospitality is the difference between a *conditional* welcome versus an *unconditional* welcome. A conditional welcome tells the guest that they can come in but must meet certain requirements for acceptance and inclusion. Some examples of the unspoken rules of a conditional welcome include: the roles of the greeter and the guest remain distinct and separate, the guest must accept and follow the rules of the house, the guest is expected to adapt to established expectations and traditions, the guest's appearance and mannerisms should not deviate from conventional practices, or the guest is not expected to stay for an inordinate amount of time. An unconditional welcome requires no such rules or limitations.

An unconditional hospitality requires a clear intention, a commitment to a lot of work and commitment, and a great degree of courage and fortitude because it literally involves opening wide all the doors of the church and encouraging the guest to become the host. Conditional hospitality is supported by display, presentation, monologue, and declamation while unconditional hospitality thrives in discussion, interaction, dialogue, and negotiation. Unconditional hospitality or radical welcoming can be disorienting and unnerving to those used to a certain pattern of behaviors but a conditional hospitality does not allow for growth and renewal.

What Radical Hospitality Is Not

As important as it is to understand the nature of Radical Hospitality it is also important to understand what it is not. For one thing, Radical Hospitality is not a convenient catch phrase. A church cannot be radically hospitable without a great deal of work and effort. This was the point in the creation of the original Welcoming Congregation Program initiated by the UUA. It could never be enough to just say that a congregation is welcoming or to put up a sign declaring the same. Designation as a Welcoming Congregation required a commitment to education about gender fluidity, intentional engagement with the congregation, and a willingness to reach out to the local community. Similarly, Radical Hospitality needs a commitment to learn about the historical oppression and marginalization of different groups of people.

Radical hospitality is also not a call to eradicate all congregational traditions or customs. It does ask that these community patterns be examined and discussed to determine whether or not they can or should be altered to allow for a greater sense of open community within the church. Some traditions may need to be replaced, some may need to be revised, and some may need to remain intact. In addition, the focus of reviewing church policies and procedures in the light of becoming more welcoming does not and should not become a time for judgment and guilt of any person involved in the process. Radical Hospitality should become a process of positive reinforcement where love and compassion flow both outward and inward. As people open their hearts to The Stranger on the outside so they also come to open their hearts to The Stranger on the inside. The one who is welcomed becomes the host and the one who welcomes becomes the guest. All open doors allow movement in both directions.

Radical Hospitality is also not a growth strategy–at least as long as the dominant culture continues to resist diversity. People who are uncomfortable with expanding the unspoken boundaries of the church's population may threaten to leave and others who harbor traditional expectations about the church might not join.

The purpose of the program is to fulfill the mission of the church in its efforts to encourage spiritual growth for all through a free and responsible search for truth and meaning. Radical Hospitality is not about numbers. It is about saving people from hatred, desolation, and intolerance.

Stephanie Spellers, the author of the book *Radical Welcome: Embracing God, the Other, and the Spirit of Transformation* and the person who coined the term 'Radical Welcome' defines the concept in her influential book.

> Radical Welcome is the spiritual practice of embracing and being changed by the gifts, presence, voices, and power of The Other: the people systematically cast out of or marginalized within a church, a denomination, and/ or society. Your church may be predominantly white or Latino, wealthy or working-class, gay or straight, middle-aged or fairly young. Regardless of your demographic profile, you still have a margin, a disempowered Other who is in your midst or just outside your door. In fact, you

may be The Other. Radical Welcome is concerned with the transformation and opening of individual hearts, congregations, and systems so that The Other might find in your community a warm place and a mutual embrace and so that you are finally free to embrace and be transformed by authentic relationship with the margins.

Chapter Two: The Radically Hospitable Church

A welcoming and hospitable church has a number of similar characteristics including a connection to the community and compassion toward strangers but a church based on Radical Hospitality has these qualities and more.

A radically hospitable church has an intention to go beyond mere welcoming. That intention includes the desire to overcome traditional patterns of dominance and oppression found in the community and in the church as well. It includes a vision of shared power and participation rather than systems of fixed hierarchical power. It sets out the goal of overcoming systemic racism.

Such a vision is not based on a short term goal but is based on a plan that reaches deep into the future toward an era of mutual equity and justice. These things are brought about by deep theological grounding in the obligation and need for Radical Hospitality. A solid theological grounding makes possible Radical Hospitality to all people through deep-rooted compassion.

The Theology of Welcoming

Religion is a human phenomenon which means that all religions will share some common themes to address some similar human needs. Major religions and their teachings must relate to the lives of humans to be relevant. Some categories of discussion (or revelation, perhaps) that are common to many, if not all the world religions, include to provide explanations and meanings to the mysteries of our existence. Some of these attempt to answer questions such as how the world began, the nature of the universe, why humans are flawed, the possibility of a higher power, why we die, and what happens to us after death. However, the topics that receive the most attention in most sacred texts are those dealing with relationships: to self, to the family, to the community of fellow worshippers, to the larger community, to place, to people of other religions, and, most importantly, to the divine.

Religious teachings are concerned about how we treat ourselves and each other. Whatever the divine principle may be, human beings are most often seen as capable (though not always fully capable) of imitating its love and compassion to some degree. This includes the so-called Golden Rule so common to religions that entreats people to engage with the one called the Stranger, the Other, or the Neighbor. Radical welcoming is a primary guiding principle of the world's religions. Doing good to others–known or unknown–is considered an act of goodness or righteousness. For many traditions, welcoming the Stranger is the same as encountering God.

All three of the Abrahamic religions (Judaism, Christianity, and Islam) began with the plight of nomadic or wandering people. Hospitality in such cultures is a survival technique and became an important way to spread the religion. The role of people in nested relationships is the central focus of Confucianism. Taoism may have been a reaction against the regimented Confucian order of relationships but it, too, places great importance on the interactions of humans as a reflection of the harmony of nature. Vedic Hinduism encourages people to see the divine reflected in all beings. Buddhism emerged from its Hindu roots to emphasize compassion and the release of both fear and desire. (See the appendices for a list of sacred texts concerning hospitality.)

Unitarian Universalists are not tied to any single traditional world religion but even humanism and naturalism (two large philosophical categories that are popular with many UUs) focus on the importance of human relationships and the acceptance of all people and beings. Unitarian Universalism also places great significance on the concept of radical hospitality not through sacred edict but through the seven (or eight) principles which guide us. Specifically, 1, 2, 3, 6, 7, and the proposed 8th principle all speak directly to the need and importance of radical welcoming. (See the Appendices for a closer look at these principles.)

Radical Hospitality as a Spiritual Practice

Radical hospitality is meant to not only change the culture of a church, it can also be a spiritual practice for individuals. Radical hospitality can change the person doing the welcoming as well as the guest. Encountering the Stranger or someone who seems different in some way can invoke fear and facing fear is also a spiritual practice. Fear can become a teacher when we become aware of what it is we fear and why. Fear is only necessary in the face of a life-threatening situation. Otherwise, fear can become a debilitating restraint on taking action. Breathing into a fear rather than running from it may reveal its source. Speaking about a fear in a safe space may bring it into the light. Only fear that is recognized, named, and acknowledged can be brought under control. Learning from fear helps to open spaces in the heart for peace and understanding.

When fear is exposed, a space is opened up for a seed of growth. Meditation, discussion, mindfulness, prayer, or other forms of practice can be used to encourage the seed to grow. Multiple seeds grown in the heart can cultivate into a regular practice of compassion–an important and necessary part of radical hospitality.

The Process

Radical hospitality involves all the members of a religious

community. It only takes one person to make another feel unwelcome or to send them away in anger or disappointment. The entire congregation can at least be in agreement of the need for Radical Hospitality so that welcoming is authentic.

The process offered here for encouraging and enacting Radical Hospitality comes in four parts: Vision, Invitation, Inclusion, and Transformation. The Vision is a process of discernment and commitment for the community. People engaged in this work should be clear about why they want to become a radically inclusive church. It is during the Vision phase that a congregation can decide if they will become an inviting congregation or a radically hospitable congregation. The difference is that the radically hospitable community allows the energy and experience of each new person to influence and enrich it. The practice invites renewal and regeneration for all involved.

The Invitation includes all the things that are done to encourage people to come to the church. It starts from the first time people look at the church's website to the moment they return home. Every step a potential newcomer takes within and beyond the church should be examined to see if it reflects and expresses the message of acceptance and inclusion the congregation has envisioned. Authenticity of intention and not just the appearance of being welcome is important.

Inclusion is the act of fully involving and including those who are new or interested in the church. It involves a process of following through with visitors so that they no longer feel like a visitor. More importantly, however, the process of inclusion is a time for listening and reflecting for both the newcomer and the congregation. Inclusion is the process of asking people to become part of a community but radical inclusion is the process of asking people to redefine the community through their presence and interaction. It is the willingness to engage in radical inclusion that leads the community toward the final stage of the process–transformation.

Transformation is the stage of the process where those who

have been invited and included are then asked to help the church further the goal of becoming a radically hospitable community. A radically hospitable church understands that change and renewal happens not only to the guest but to the host as well. Each new person should then become part of the conversation on how the church can become even more welcoming and, subsequently, relevant to the lives of every member of the congregation–new or not.

Chapter Three: Welcoming The Stranger

R adical Hospitality begins with a vision of how a church wants to fulfill its mission. Hopefully, that mission includes the need to be open to the inclusion of the stranger and the desire to be revitalized through each encounter. Fulfilling that mission can be done through a process of discernment, review, and change. That process should include the steps of Visioning, Invitation, Inclusion, and Transformation.

Visioning

The first step of making any change in a church is to create a vision and a plan through its leadership. A new initiative may come from the work of a subcommittee, task force, or some other ad hoc body of people within the church but, eventually, the leadership should be involved and take the lead.

One of the first steps to the Visioning step should be to become aware of the current situation. To know where to go it helps to know where you are starting. What are the current attitudes in the church about welcoming and hospitality? Where is the impetus for Radical Hospitality coming from? How is it being received?

Through a series of compassionate conversations the leadership might consider crafting a vision for the church. Why would your church need to do this work? How do you envision the effect that radical hospitality would have on the life of the congregation? What other effects might such a change have on the church? (See the Visioning Questions on the Appendices for a more complete list.)

Once a vision has been defined by the leadership then it can be brought before the congregation. Conversations about radical hospitality can be done in small groups, cottage meetings, or other formal and informal gatherings. The focus of these conversations should be on a clear understanding of what radical hospitality is and what it is not, why radical hospitality is important, and the vision of how it might be implemented.

After a time the concept can be introduced and explored through a service dedicated to it. Radical Hospitality, after all, will only be effective if a large part of the congregation is behind the vision and is willing to both make the effort and be willing to be transformed. The service can include ways in which all the members can become aware of their role in the process and how it can be implemented.

Welcoming Teams

Once the congregation has made a commitment to Radical Hospitality, teams of people may be assembled and made aware of how each can make an effective contribution to the effort. Some of the volunteer teams can include a committee or team dedicated to the implementation of the vision, as well as greeters, ushers, and ambassadors.

The Welcoming or Hospitality Committee can be the group of people who coordinate the entire program. Their responsibilities can include:

- Train the volunteers in the concept of Radical Hospitality.
- Identify and track visitors and new people to the church.
- Coordinate communications to visitors including initial contacts and follow-up connections.
- Set up and maintain an effective Information Center.
- Coordinate the Church Members Center.
- Coordinate after-worship events for visitors such as

coffee hour.

- Review the church and grounds for hospitality effectiveness.

The Greeters are often the first people that visitors first encounter. They can:

- Greet people at the door for services and other events.
- Identify visitors and new people.
- Guide people to specific locations in the church.
- Be a source of curiosity and interest in current members and visitors.
- Be a source of information when requested.

The Ushers oversee what happens inside the sanctuary space during services or other events. They can:

- (Before the service:)
  - In coordination with the worship team, prepare the space to be used.
  - Hand out bulletins, orders of service, programs, or other sources of information about the service.
  - Help participants find a seat and get comfortable.
- (During the service:)
  - Assist the worship team in coordinating activities with the participants, if needed.
  - Collect the Offering.
  - Maintain a safe and respectful atmosphere in the sanctuary.
  - Be prepared for any possible threat to the health and safety of all participants.
- (After the service:)
  - Provide directions to the Coffee Hour space or other events after the service to visitors.
  - Help restore order and cleanliness to the space.
  - Count and dispense the Offering donations according to church policy.

Ambassadors are people who volunteer to visit or host newcomers. They can:

- Contact visitors who have expressed an interest in learning more about the church (Friends).
- Offer to host or make a visit to Friends.
- Act as a liaison to the church for Friends.
- Help Friends make connections with others in the church.

The Radical Hospitality Committee

The Radical Hospitality Committee needs to be fully invested in the concept of Radical Hospitality and its premise of inviting and including all people in a process of mutual transformation. Radical Hospitality is deeply connected to principles of counter-oppression, social justice, intersectionality, and deep listening. A basic understanding of each of these principles and how they influence the local community of the church and potential visitors is key to the success of the program. The committee can both understand these concepts and be able to pass on these key issues to all aspects of a Radical Hospitality program.

The committee can keep current information and records about people who visit the church, what they may seek or need, and how their requests or needs were met. This information helps ensure that those who have expressed an interest in the church are not ignored or forgotten. Such information might include a record of all communications attempted, received, and answered.

The committee can be in charge of establishing and maintaining an Information Center for visitors. The Information Center is a place where people can quickly and easily get small amounts of information about the church, Unitarian-Universalism, important places within the church, and what a visitor or new member should know. There can also be a Members Center with name tags for all the church members. Other information in a Members Center can include a calendar of upcoming events and services, local stories of interest, and committee and team memberships.

Although there is often a separate committee that provides coffee, tea, and snacks after each service, the Radical Hospitality Committee might also have some involvement with Coffee Hour. The Coffee Team could be a subcommittee of the Welcome Committee but, either way, consistency is important in the message given to newcomers. The Coffee Team needs to operate with the same counter-oppressive and open listening techniques as the Radical Hospitality Committee.

The Welcoming Committee can also make regular reviews of the facilities and practices to make sure that the goals of Radical Hospitality are being met.

Greeters

Greeters are often the first person a visitor encounters when coming to the church. Greeters provide the setting for the rest of the visit. As the name suggests, Greeters acknowledge visitors with acceptance and appreciation. They are both an immediate friend and a guide to all who enter. They receive new visitors and bring them into the church's protocol for newcomers. They direct and sometimes accompany people toward important locations within the church such as the sanctuary or the location for Coffee Hour. They are genuinely curious people who want to know the condition and disposition of every person who walks through the front door and they are happy to provide answers to questions about the community, the building, and the faith tradition.

Ushers

Ushers focus on the sanctuary space before, during, and after worship. They help to prepare the sanctuary and to make sure that people are comfortably seated for the service. They often hand out bulletins or orders of service. Anything that goes on in the seating area is the purview of the ushers including the health and safety of all those in attendance at the worship service.

Ambassadors

Ambassadors are volunteers who make a special commitment to newcomers who have identified that they want to learn more about a spiritual community (identified here as Friends). Ambassadors can host a meal or a simple gathering such as the sharing of tea or coffee at their home or another gathering location. During such a gathering and subsequent visits, Ambassadors become a liaison between Friends and the rest of the congregation. Just like Greeters and Ushers, Ambassadors need to understand how to engage with Friends using the principles of Radical Welcoming. Ambassadors help Friends to tell their stories and explore what they seek or need rather than work to indoctrinate or inculcate them.

Chapter Four: Invitation

O nce a goal of Radical Hospitality has been envisioned and a commitment has been made toward the fulfillment of that vision, preparation can begin for inviting people into it. Every aspect related to how someone will first encounter the community can be reviewed in terms of the goals of Radical Hospitality. Specifically each part of a newcomer's experience can be scrutinized with the following questions:

- Is it easy for anyone (of any ability or any background) to find and access?

- Is it easy for anyone to navigate?

- Does it encourage the participation of anyone as their own true and authentic self?

- Does it lead to further exploration and realization of the mission and goals of the church?

If someone cannot easily find and access what they need to enter they will not take the time and energy to do so. It takes a great deal of stamina and fortitude to enter into a new space with new people. People do not expend such energy unless they believe there is something worthwhile from investing in it. If the level of energy put into the effort does not lead to anything of value to the newcomer they will simply leave and, most likely, not return. Things and places need to be easily found and simple to navigate (both physically and mentally).

Part of the concept of Radical Hospitality is that the true and authentic self of the newcomer is invited to fully participate in the community and their participation is encouraged to transform it in the process. No part of the program should ask the newcomer to adapt to determined habits or standards. The goal of a Radical Hospitality program cannot be to move people toward conformity. Rather, the objective needs to be focused on the universality of the unique worth, dignity, and value of every person and the power of a sacred beloved community to provide healing, meaning, and joy in life. The Radical Hospitality program is a means toward developing this kind of sacred community. Every part of the program should be designed to open a door to a further and deeper exploration of spirituality and the meaning of a sacred community.

The Website

The first place that almost everyone looks for information about a church even before they enter the front door is on its web page. If the home page of a website is not in itself inviting and welcoming then people will simply look elsewhere. Unfortunately, many websites are not geared towards newcomers but are focused instead on the current membership. The first page of any website should be focused on the guest first. Information for members and staff can be found at a deeper level where those people will know where to obtain the information they need. A good rule of thumb to remember is that everything a guest may want to know should be available within three clicks or less. Most people will leave a webpage if they cannot find what they seek within a few taps.

Consider having the web page professionally designed. In the same way that a church building is constructed from professional architects and built by professional contractors a website needs to have the same consideration to become a clean, well-designed, and useful source of information. Even if professionally designed, it is important to make sure that the web page has everything needed to make it useful and inviting.

The Home Page is the first page a visitor sees when they load the church's web address. On that Home Page can be several virtual tabs or buttons that lead to additional pages. It is important not to try and put too much information on the Home Page or it will look cluttered and be difficult to navigate. On the other hand, it is also a good idea not to have too many tabs. Think of the information as interconnected pathways-the more there are, the easier it is to get lost.

The Home Page can have basic information and pathways to find further particulars. It should at least contain the following: a welcome message, a clear statement of worship times, clear directions on how to get to the church, contact information, and an assurance of safety. The page can also include good quality and inviting photography of people enjoying themselves together in the church or on the grounds. Overall, the page should be enjoyable to view and free of distractions.

The Welcome Statement can be a short paragraph welcoming visitors to the page and inviting them to the church. Often, such a welcome is written by the senior minister and expresses a joy for expressing an interest in the church. The statement can include a very brief introduction to Unitarian Universalism and the church itself with a welcoming invitation for every person of any faith, identity, or background.

Once people feel welcomed and are interested in coming to a service they need to know when the service begins and how to get to it. Worship times can be clearly listed. The address of the church should be included with links to mapping applications that can help them find their way. Visitors can be told that further information is available on a particular tab designed to help people plan their first visit.

Visitors will want to quickly find basic contact information in case they have specific questions or want to make a first contact before visiting. This contact information can include an office phone number, the church's general email address, basic information on getting any regular correspondence like a church newsletter or weekly email, and any social media links related to the church.

It is also important to have some basic information that

assures people that visits to the church are safe for visitors and their children. Information about procedures concerning any illness that may affect the community and statements about inclusion in the UUA Safe Congregations program or similar practices should also be clear and visible. Some people will choose not to visit without these assurances.

A few photos are also important to the overall feeling and attractiveness of the page. Pictures can include a shot of the church building clearly showing its front entrance (preferably open) and a few photos of past events. It is important that some or all of the photos include people who look happy to be present and part of a loving and warm community.

Home Page Tabs

On the Home page there can be clearly placed tabs or buttons that visitors can use to get further information. Fewer buttons is better but there must be enough to lead people to all the information that both visitors, friends, members, and staff may need to obtain. Consider at least the following five tabs:

- Our Church
- Worship
- Ministry
- Plan A Visit
- Members

The "Our Church" tab can lead to a page that provides even more information from the Home Page. Material can include a more in-depth description of Unitarian Universalism including basic premises, some history, the Principles, and the Sources. Copies of specific church documents such as its Covenant and its Mission Statement can either be on the page or easily accessible. Another link can be added that leads to information, contact links, and photos of the church staff. An important part of the page should include what it means to be a member of the church and specific information about how someone can join.

The "Worship" tab can contain information and links to any activity related to services for the community. Sunday services can be explained and a list of past and future themes and topics can be included. A typical Sunday service with an order of service that represents what happens on most Sundays can help visitors feel less out of place when joining. Special services like Vespers, Pagan circles, Buddhist meditations, Soulful Sundays, etc. can be listed with links for further exploration. Information about accessibility features and policies should also be clearly stated.

The "Ministry" tab can contain links to pages that describe all the ways in which the church serves its members, friends, visitors, and local and global communities. These are the specific ministries the church supports and each can probably fill its own page with useful knowledge including its purpose, philosophy, history, and examples of its good work. Those pages can be mentioned and linked through one central page. The ministries of a UU church typically include Music, Arts, Religious Education, Social Justice, Pastoral Care, Small Group ministry, the Worship Team, and other outreach programs.

The "Plan A Visit" tab is geared specifically to visitors. Its goal is to help visitors feel as comfortable as possible about their first visit to the church. A visitor should know what to expect at a typical service including what happens before, during, and after the service; the average length of the service; what people usually wear; and what is provided and expected for children. Visitors can learn that there will be Greeters and Ushers there to help them find their way. Information about accessibility and safety is often sought by visitors. Directions to the church and information about parking and alternative transportation is also often needed for a visitor to make it to the church. Consider also adding a link to a page with frequently asked questions (sometimes called the FAQ page). These are questions that are often received by the front office or staff. Placing their answers on the web page anticipates some common concerns of visitors.

The "Members" page is where information is placed that

would probably not be of interest to visitors. A members' directory, a listing of committees and their progress, news articles or websites, and links to other important documents and information can be made available quickly for members without interfering with a visitor's search.

The Facilities

Once someone has been impressed and intrigued by the website, they may decide to become an in-person visitor. Just like the web page needs to be fully welcoming and inviting, so does the church and the grounds they have come to visit. The first thing most people will encounter is the parking lot. Many churches–especially urban churches–do not have enough parking and the few spaces that are available on a Sunday morning are often filled by the members who come early to prepare the church for service. By the time visitors arrive, many of the parking spaces are not available. To be fully welcoming, a parking lot should have handicap spaces and handicap accessibility to the front entrance. Several other spaces can also be reserved specifically for visitors. If a parking lot does get filled, it may be necessary to designate overflow parking in other spaces which would require that directions to those spaces are made easily available. Visitors who cannot easily find a parking spot will simply drive away.

Parking lots often include signs that designate special places and directions. This kind of clear signage needs to be applied throughout the grounds and the buildings. Signs in the parking lot can help someone find a place to park and then show them how to get to the front door. Any pathways to the front should be clean and accessible to people of all abilities or some assistance should be made available.

The front entrance of the church should be clear and easy for anyone to access. Hopefully, visitors will have seen a picture of it on the website but that should not be necessary for anyone to quickly identify its location. A clear, inviting, and beautifully designed sign can help anyone be able to identify the front entrance. A Greeter at the front door also adds to the sense that one has entered a warm and friendly space. Visitors can be encouraged (though never forced) to write their name on a temporary name tag so that others can identify that they are a visitor and can welcome them.

At the very least, a person who walks through the front door should be able to quickly find the bathrooms, the Fellowship Hall (or wherever Coffee Hour is held), and the Sanctuary without any help. This information can be given through simple and clear signs or maps made even more accessible through the addition of braille, additional languages, and inclusive terminology. Inversely, visitors should be able to find their way back to the front entrance or the other locations with the same kind of directions. Some churches have added television monitors throughout the building which can act as a large map as well as a provider of relevant news and information.

Once a visitor arrives at the sanctuary for service they should encounter a clean, well-lit, and fully audible space where they can be comfortable and able to fully participate in a service regardless of any disability (visible or not), condition, or identity. Again, some churches have adopted the use of a television monitor inside the sanctuary to aid people in seeing text, hymns, and other visual aids useful throughout the service. For sound, hearing devices can be made available through the use of a wireless sound system.

One thing that is often missing in UU sanctuary spaces is a symbol of what Unitarian Universalism represents. It is quite obvious when the one enters the sacred space of a Catholic Church, a Jewish synagogue, or a Muslim mosque. Each is filled with religious symbolism and artifacts important to their respected faith. When a visitor enters a sacred space they may be able to experience that sense of reverence regardless of their own religious background. Without some basic symbolism and imagery there may be little difference between a sanctuary and a performance space like an auditorium or theater. Some people have joined a UU church because they saw a banner on the wall that displayed a collection of symbols of religions from around the world. Sanctuaries are often wonderful spaces for displaying art that reflects UU principles including representations of the flaming chalice and rainbow images of inclusivity.

The Information Center

As introduced earlier, an important site for visitors is the Information Center. This is a location in the church where visitors can quickly access more information about the church, its mission, and its programs. Preferably, the Information Center can be wherever visitors are urged to enter but space limitations may eliminate such a possibility. In this case, directions from the entrance to the Information Center can be easily accessible and clear in maps and signs. It is important to have enough information to help a visitor understand the church and its mission but not too much information that might overwhelm them.

Basic information for an Information Center can be provided through clear, well-designed, and colorful pamphlets (available from the UUA) or printed sheets that include information about the church, about Unitarian Universalism, and how a visitor can become more active or join the church. Maps of the building, newsletters, and minimal information about the various ministries can also be made available. An important function of the Information Center is to make it possible for visitors to express an interest in learning more about the church. There can be a stack of small and brief Contact Cards and cards that request a more permanent name tag. Consider including some pencils or pens so that people can fill out those information cards.

The permanent name tags can be important sources of information for visitors. They, of course, display the name of the wearer but can include further information such as gender pronoun preferences or specific roles such as Greeter or Usher. The color of the name tag can relate to particular ministries of the church. Colored ribbons, pins, or stickers can identify specific roles, memberships, or interests. Using colored name tags with titles or pins can help visitors quickly identify greeters, ushers, staff, board members, the RE team, the music team, or other people who they may want to find.

In another part of the church or near but separate from the Information Center can be placed the Members Center. This is the place where members and friends of the church can find their permanent name tags. The Members Center can also include information, announcements, and news specific to the church members and the local community.

In many UU churches membership is not a requirement for someone to switch from wearing temporary name tags to the more permanent (comparatively) plastic name tag. However, membership is a privilege and an honor and can be demonstrated on the permanent name tag as an encouragement for others to join the church. A chalice sticker or something similar can be placed on the permanent name tag to identify those who are members of the church.

Another area or areas throughout the church that can be important to Radical Hospitality are the walls and open spaces themselves. Art by local artists including by traditionally oppressed artists can help people feel recognized and included. If the church has an art space, consider sponsoring shows that explore issues of inclusivity. Art that expresses UU principles with messages of openness and compassion can be placed in many places throughout the church. Other forms of art can be employed to do the same. Poetry and stories of Radical Hospitality can be shared, music from oppressed voices can be performed, and other forms of performing and fine art can convey messages of invitation and inclusion.

The Greeters

Greeters and Ushers are the most visible and, arguably, the most important element of a complete Radical Hospitality program. Greeters are often the first people that visitors meet at the front door or even in the parking lot. Their function is to make both new people and long-time members feel welcome and appreciated and to make sure people get to where they are going.

Greeters will be the first ones to identify the presence of a visitor. The first few seconds of that initial greeting can determine whether or not a visitor will return. In the context of Radical Hospitality it is important that the Greeter meet the person where they are (both literally and metaphorically). The visitor must feel comfortable and appreciated for who they are and not who the church might want them to be. People are not numbers to be used to fill quotas or membership goals. They are souls seeking their own truth and spiritual fulfillment. Greeters can be the first ones to open up that important space where people can begin to find what they seek. Greeters can initiate a conversation that is meant more to hear the visitor speak than to inform them about the church. In that brief encounter, the Greeter takes a genuine interest in the uniqueness and sacredness of the visitor.

Such a conversation may begin with understanding the level of engagement a visitor wants to pursue. Some people prefer to enter a sacred space silently without initially making any contacts. A preference for isolation should be respected in visitors just as much as there may be preference by others to reach out. Initial eye contact is often the first key to predicting the level of comfort a visitor may have with new people.

Greeters can offer the visitor who seeks it the opportunity to be recognized through the use of a temporary name tag. The temporary name tag is often a sticker and appears differently from a permanent name tag which makes it easier for members to take notice. If interested, the visitor can be shown the Information Center and asked if they would like to fill out a Contact Card. Next, the visitor can be guided to the worship space where the Usher can then take over.

The most obvious and important location for a Greeter is, of course, the front door but if there are enough volunteers in the Greeter Team, consider having some additional Greeters placed throughout the church. One of the most important and often neglected areas of making an initial impression of a church is in its parking lot. If a visitor cannot easily find a parking space–especially if they have any particular accessibility needs–they will simply turn around and drive away. A Greeter in the parking lot (assuming the weather is not too intolerable) can help direct people to open parking spaces or to spaces in overflow lots and can guide them toward the entrance. They can also offer or request further aid to those who may need assistance to get to the church. Most importantly, they can offer a warm smile to someone who is probably feeling confused and uncertain about where they should go and what they should do in a new space.

At least one Greeter is often at the front door but consider having at least two at the entrance, if possible. If one Greeter is showing a guest to the worship space and another visitor appears at the door, there will be no one to greet that person. Another possibility is to include on the team a special Greeter known as a Floating Greeter who spends their time moving throughout the church to make sure that everyone is getting to where they want to go and to offer any assistance needed throughout the building.

Finally, if possible, add a Greeter to the Coffee Hour fellowship after the service. The purpose of this Greeter is to make sure that visitors (especially those with temporary name tags) are introduced to people and are made to feel welcomed. The Greeter can encourage conversations between members and visitors. Often visitors who make it to Coffee Hour find themselves separated and alone because the members form themselves into groups of familiar faces. Hopefully, the congregation has been informed about the principles of Radical Hospitality and will allow the visitor to bring themselves into the conversation and be recognized for who they are as unique individuals. Being willing to be in full relationship with a visitor is more effective than any sort of marketing.

The Ushers

Ushers take responsibility for the sanctuary space during

worship. They help to prepare the space, offer assistance during the service where congregants are involved, assure health and comfort for everyone, and help put the sanctuary back in order after the service. Consider letting the Ushers hand out the Order of Service instead of the Greeters so that Greeters are free to help show people around the church and offer assistance. There should be at least one Usher at each entrance to the sanctuary. Ushers can be on the lookout for visitors with temporary name tags so that they can be given extra guidance on where to sit. Most long-time members will have their own favorite seats but visitors will not know where to sit and may feel awkward walking into the sanctuary. Ushers can also answer questions about the service as they guide people to their seats. In the same manner as the Greeters, Ushers need to be able to open a space for the visitor to express themselves and their needs.

Both Ushers and Greeters serve a similar function and, therefore, need to understand and practice some similar protocols in order to be most effective in their goal of making all people feel invited and welcome.

Below are three basic tips for appearance and six basic tips for interaction that Ushers and Greeters can use in their interactions with visitors.

Tips For Appearance

1. Fresh clothes
2. Fresh breath
3. Fresh air

Appearance is important for a visitor. Although a formal outfit is not necessary, wearing something clean and attractive gives the impression that the Usher and Greeter take seriously their purpose and want to make a good impression. Just as the clothes need to be appealing and clean so the person wearing them should be free of distracting smells or odors. Heavy amounts of perfume or cologne can be distracting or even disturbing to those who may be allergic to strong odors.

Tips For Interaction

1. Smile

2. Make eye contact

3. Take the initiative

4. Say your name

5. Ask them what they need

6. Enjoy the experience

A smile is the most important act of both Ushers and Greeters. For people who may not have seen a smile in a long time, a simple act of kindness through the projection of an authentic smile can go a long way.

Secondly, eye contact helps to establish a connection and the return of eye contact is important information to the Usher and Greeter. Those who return eye contact often want to make a connection and are usually open to further interaction while those who avoid eye contact should not be pushed to interact any further. Those who avoid eye contact often may also shun verbal or physical contact. No visitor should ever be pushed beyond their own level of comfort since the goal of a hospitality program is to make people feel comfortable.

Of course, giving the first smile and offering eye contact requires some initiative but the Usher and the Greeter need to go beyond these two things if the visitor has signaled a desire to be welcomed further. Because visitors are naturally shy at first the Greeter and the Usher need to take the next step and make an introduction. The introduction can include the announcement of a name followed by a chance for the visitor to reveal what they hope to find through their experience.

The natural tendency is then to tell the visitor all about the church and how they can fit in if they so desire. Radical Inclusion asks that this be avoided and, instead, the visitor should be given the chance to explain what it is they need in their spiritual journey and what they hope to find in a sacred community.

Finally, the experience between Visitors, Greeters, and Ushers should be an enjoyable one for all. Visitors will appreciate the pleasure of meeting people who take great joy engaging with others.

The Order of Service

The Program, Bulletin, or Order of Service (OOS) is often the first printed piece of information that visitors see. It is important that it be kept simple and easy to read. It can contain the basic information of what will happen in the service and any information needed to participate in that service without being overfilled and distracting. Besides the service information, the OOS can include some basic contact information, the church web page address, and some basic information on how to get further involved in the church.

The OOS also needs to be fully accessible for every visitor and member. Braille and large print versions of a basic format can be made available. Another way to make both options available is through the use of a digital version of the OOS that can be quickly accessed from a printed web address or a posted QR code. Of course, not everyone uses smartphone and tablet technology but an increasing number of people do and are quite comfortable with getting their information in this way. Digital information can be changed much easier than printed information and the user can change the font size or add vocalizations of the words for better access.

The Service

Since UU worship services vary so much between congregations and locations, not much will be said about them except for two important points: language and the wording of the Welcome.

The worship service is the point where most visitors who may have felt welcomed into the church will make their decision about whether they want to return. The worship service is where the church reveals what is important to them, why those things are important, and how people should live their lives in relation to them. People should feel invited into this sense of how UUs view the world.

The language used on the service needs to be as inviting and welcoming as the rest of the experience. Language can be made inclusive at every instance. Insider language that identifies groups or people with nicknames or short cuts can either be avoided or explained. Language that is oppressive or appears to favor one type of people over another should be avoided or explained (as in when an ancient text is used). In short, all language can be reviewed to make sure that it invites people in rather than separating them.

Arguably the most important part of the service as far as hospitality is concerned is the beginning of the service or the section sometimes just called the Welcome. Consider including the following elements in your worship service Welcome or Introduction.

- A basic greeting that includes the name of your church and your denomination.
- A greeting to visitors
- A statement about accessibility and safety.
- The names of your worship leaders.
- A brief statement about the beliefs and the mission of the church.
- A brief statement about the values of Unitarian Universalism

- Information on how to find out more about the church.

- The location and purpose of Coffee Hour and how to get there.

The importance of the Introduction or Welcome to visitors and a hospitality program can be easily overlooked. It is not as spiritually significant as the prayer or the sermon but is the first thing that visitors hear and can set the tone for the rest of the service. The Welcome can be the difference between a service meant only for the members of the church and a service open to all. Visitors need to know that they are truly welcome and should feel comfortable about what goes on in the rest of the service. It helps them to know if there are ways to meet any accessibility needs, who they can talk to in order to get more information, and where they go to join in fellowship after the service. Another thing that visitors are looking for when they come to a new church is that they want to hear what the church is about. They have come to the church not just to meet new people but to be enriched spiritually. They want to know if the theology of the church and its practices meet with their own spiritual understanding–whatever that may be at the time of their visit.

The Congregation

The largest and possibly the most important component of a successful Radical Hospitality program is the congregation itself. It is important that all members of the church understand how to apply the open and listening approach of Radical Hospitality. Being welcoming to visitors involves everyone. The entire congregation needs to be aware of the presence of any visitor and consider themselves part of a larger welcoming committee.

People tend to cluster together into groups of familiar faces and contiguous dialogues which can isolate visitors. The congregation can be encouraged to feel empowered and comfortable with the idea of inviting unknown people into conversations. Those conversations can open a space for the new person to share their story. In practical terms, every single person a visitor encounters should be able to act as a Greeter to them.

The most important points the congregation as a whole should understand:

- Everyone is a Greeter.

- Pay attention to new faces and temporary name tags.

- Be flexible with visitors about gathering and attending service.

- Pay attention to clusters.

In a truly radically hospitable church of any moderate or greater size, a small group of Greeters cannot be expected to be the only ones who seek out and welcome visitors. All the members of the church are Greeters. During coffee hour and other events members can be on the lookout for people wearing temporary name tags or who may be unfamiliar. A simple personal introduction or an introduction to another member may be all that is needed. Sometimes this vigilance will require that people pay attention to the tendency to cluster into groups of familiarity. Talking with people we know and love is one of the many reasons people come to church but such pods of people can be intimidating to those who are unknown.

Chapter Five: Inclusion

T he Radical Hospitality program goes on even after the first visit from a guest. We want people to feel welcome and invited to join the church in its mission to build a truly beloved community. In other words, we want them to come back and consider becoming an active member.

The Follow-Through

First time visitors are identified at the door and given the opportunity to explore further by taking on a temporary name tag so that others will approach them and by going to the Information Center and filling out a Contact Card. Visitors are not required to do either of these things and should never feel pressured or intimidated to do so.

Visitors who take these steps, however, do want further contact and they should not be disappointed in the opportunity. A working system can be set up to process the Contact Cards and initiate a follow-up note or letter within only a few days from when the visitor arrived at the front door. That note does not have to be long but it should be personal and pleasant. It is basically a thank-you note with an invitation to return or contact the church for more information or interaction.

The Ambassador Program

It is easy for visitors to get lost in the shuffle and bustle of a busy church year. There is always something else for which to prepare, rehearse, plan, present, and so on. A new face and a new name can be easily overlooked. That is why it is important to follow-through with correspondence but an additional level of follow-through can be done on a more personal level through an

Ambassador program. Ambassadors are members of the church who have submitted their names as volunteers and who are assigned to specific people new to the church. Ambassadors can be individuals, families, or small groups. Their goal is to become a liaison between visitors and members. Ambassadors help to ensure that no one is forgotten or ignored.

Once a visitor has indicated that they would like more contact from the church, the Ambassador connects with that person or family and either asks to come visit them where they live or invites the visitor to their home for coffee, tea, or a simple meal. During that time, the principles of Radical Hospitality can be applied. The purpose of the discussion during the gathering is not to convince, cajole, or coerce anyone into joining or doing anything at the church. Rather, the aim for Ambassadors hosting a discussion is to listen fully and deeply to the visitor and to answer questions openly and honestly. The Ambassador is as much a pastoral position as it is a welcoming role. Every member of a UU church is a pastor of sorts and those who reach out to visitors and guests are ministering as much as they are administering.

Beyond that initial gathering and assuming the visitors continue to return to the church, the Ambassador can then further assist the visitors. Ambassadors can help them find their way through the church, aid in getting their children involved, make introductions to other people in the church, find ways to help them pursue their interests and needs, or help out in any other appropriate way. In short, they help make the transition between guest to member easier and smoother. Ambassadors can be an important way to help people pursue their church interests through volunteer work and ministry.

Inviting People In

In many churches and other volunteer organizations there is a constant flow of people in and out of committees, task forces, the governing board, and other important volunteer activities that go on throughout the year. Often, the easiest way to fill those vacancies is to ask someone already known in the church who has previously demonstrated their skill and devotion to volunteer. While this practice may fulfill necessary positions it can preclude those who have not had a chance to demonstrate their capabilities and enthusiasm. In other words, it makes it difficult for new people to become involved in church ministries beyond the Sunday service. This can be especially true with opportunities and positions of leadership such as the membership of the church governing board.

The best way to promote participation in volunteer activities in the church for visitors, friends, and new members as part of a program in Radical Hospitality is to be completely transparent in the operations of all committee and volunteer activities. People need to know what committees are doing, what positions are needed, and what those positions require in terms of time and commitment. People interested in volunteer opportunities need to know the purpose, function, and activities of each sponsoring body as well as its current needs. That information can be shared with links to the Members Page on the website, at the Members Center in the church, or in newsletters and other distributed information.

Another way to promote volunteer activity is to sponsor a Volunteer Fair on a regular basis. The Volunteer Fair is a chance for all committees and other affiliated groups within the church (and possibly within the local community) to present information about their activities and functions within the church in a manner that allows interested people to choose and compare without feeling pressure to join. Volunteer fairs can also be a lot of fun with the addition of food, music, games, and kids activities.

Some churches offer classes for newcomers that help to introduce them to Unitarian Universalism and to the church. Some classes are specifically for newcomers while other classes help members learn to become more intentional in their participation with the church. Regular classes can include information for those new to Unitarian Universalism and classes for members who want to learn how to get more involved with their church.

Radical Inclusion

Radical Hospitality can become the foundation for Radical Inclusion by applying the same core concepts. The commitment to being open and welcoming to every person who walks into the space, a commitment to accessibility and openness, and a dedication to sacred listening can also be beacons of guidance for ongoing activities such as meetings, events, and other gatherings in the church.

Radical Inclusion is based on the concept that all activities within an inclusive church are based on models of equitable sharing of power and involvement. The difference between Radical Inclusion and the traditional model of committee work is between the top-down pyramid structure of operations to a more equanimous format. This can be done with several tools some of which include:

- The use of an inclusive meeting covenant.
- The development and use of collaborative agendas.
- The sharing of roles.
- The sharing of voices.
- The sharing of ideas.

Unitarian Universalist churches are covenantal rather than creedal. We work together based on shared principles and promises in work that is meant for the greater good. Unlike for-profit corporations, churches work to improve the world and its relationships. Our bottom line is not profits but people in relationship. We work to strengthen the web of interdependence for the sake of all beings. One way to move toward that higher purpose is to work together in the spirit of right relationship. Covenants are a way to remind us of that goal.

The Meeting Covenant

A covenant is a voluntary mutual and active agreement between members of a group of people who desire to be fully engaged in right relationship with each other. Its purpose is to prioritize the relationships of a group over its purpose. The human bond of love and compassion developed in the church should never be sacrificed in a meeting or activity in order to pursue an achievement. If that goal is not achieved through mutual respect and compassion then it is not truly earned and it can injure the mission of the church itself. A covenant is a commitment to act in the way we would hope the whole world would behave.

A covenant needs to be more than just a set of promises or a spoken contract of rules. It can list a brief set of preferred actions and attitudes but can also include why it exists and how it relates to the mission of the church in its introduction. Its inner content often has three main components that emphasize respect, right relationship, and responsibility.

Members of a covenantal group need to have respect for every one of its members regardless of experience, position, background, or the length of time spent on the committee or in church. Respect is based on an attitude of openness with an emphasis on listening more than speaking. That openness includes being willing to listen to different ideas regardless of how they may or may not follow the customs and habits of the organization or from whom they originate. In speaking, the focus is on expressing thoughts and ideas from a personal non-judgmental stance.

A covenant helps to remind members of a group to focus first on right relationships with each other. Members assume that every person in the group has come to the meeting or event for the purpose of helping the church fulfill its mission. For the most part, people who volunteer for church organizations come with good intentions even if some of their actions do not reflect it. Starting from a place of good intent helps to avoid harmful assumptions. The group assumes that people begin the meeting or activity already in right relationship. Any harmful intent or purpose will be revealed the moment a covenant is broken. At that point, the resumption of right relations is the highest priority of any covenanted group and trumps any other stated purpose. On the other hand, praise and gratitude offered genuinely and with affection can solidify the bonds of the group even during challenging moments.

The true strength of any covenantal group will be found in the depth of responsibility found in each member. Each individual can commit to doing the work they agreed to do while also asking for and offering help whenever it is needed. Responsibility also includes the ability to admit to making mistakes and to making reparations, if possible. This is especially true in the role of maintaining right relations.

The Collaborative Agenda

Many groups use an agenda to set out the areas of concern for the meeting. An agenda is important in helping to keep a meeting focused and on track. The traditional model for meetings is for the facilitator of the meeting to set the agenda beforehand and deliver it to the committee at the meeting. This does not allow much input from the rest of the group. A collaborative agenda asks for input from the entire committee before the group meets and offers ways to adjust the agenda both before and at the beginning of the meeting. An agreement on the agenda can be the first thing a meeting can vote upon.

Sharing Roles

It is also possible to share the leadership responsibilities of the group rather than using only one person consistently throughout the year. Leadership can be shared and other roles in the group can be rotated. Some members may be in charge of individual agenda items or established goals. Some functions often relegated to one chairperson can be offered to other members of the group.

Such roles can include a timekeeper, a record keeper, a moderator of voices, a person who can offer opening and closing words that help set the tone of the meeting, and a meeting monitor or someone whose task it is to check on the disposition of the participants.

Sharing Voices

The need to have all voices and ideas heard and respected is as important in the overall agenda as are the specific items in discussion. The heart of right relationship is the equal sharing of voices and compassion for all members. Whether it is the chairperson or another member of the committee, some focus of the meeting can be to make sure that all voices have a chance to speak and be heard in a respectful manner. Perhaps this equilibrium of voices and a concern for the well being of each member of the group during the meeting can be the responsibility of a person chosen specifically for these purposes. This person can direct the conversation by ensuring that no person may speak twice without at least offering everyone else the chance to express themselves. The same or a different person can monitor the reactions and moods of the members to focus on any intended or unintended harm caused. That person would then ask that the meeting be paused until right relations could be re-established.

Meetings, of course, are not the only place where voices can be heard and ideas can be shared. Worship services can reflect the people who are there to worship and different voices can be invited to join in but hearing different voices and seeing different viewpoints can be done with great effect through the sharing of art. Art is an expression of the people who make it and that expression is designed to be shared with others. Visual art that tells the stories of those who have been traditionally marginalized or oppressed through things like paintings, drawings, sculpture, or fabrics can be shared throughout the church building while performances of music, poetry, dance, or plays can bring to life important stories and viewpoints that have long been forgotten or ignored.

Chapter Six: Transformation

T he mark of true Radical Hospitality is in how it can transform a congregation. Assimilating new people into long-standing patterns ensures that there will be no changes and that the current system will not evolve. To be transformed is to be shaped in process. The process is what creates the change and as the process continues, the change increases until a positive feedback loop develops. As more and more people are brought into the church they are encouraged to bring in their full selves and, in turn, help reshape the church to make it more welcoming for others.

Reviews

Part of a positive feedback process needed to make Radical Hospitality transformational is to enact regular reviews of the church's welcoming procedures with an eye toward always making them more invitational and relational. All parts of the welcoming process can be reviewed for accuracy, accessibility, and inclusivity including images, language, web pages, signage, printed materials, and any other items shown to the public. A regular review of the process can continuously question the effectiveness of the program in relation to the program's goals and the church's mission.

Another way to review the effectiveness of a hospitality program is through the use of a "Secret Guest" program. A Secret Guest is someone unfamiliar with the church or even unfamiliar with Unitarian Universalism who is asked to visit the church and then submit a report afterwards about their experience. The Secret Guest can be given specific or more generic questions to help them review the space and the manner in which they were treated. (Some suggestions for review questions can be found in the appendix.)

An important aspect of the Secret Guest program is that the reviewer should do their work without the knowledge of anyone in the church except, perhaps, for a very few people who organized their appearance at the church. The Secret Guest might act and appear as any other newcomer would when visiting a new church.

Visibility

A Radical Hospitality program needs to be focused not only on its internal processes and procedures but on its external outreach as well. If the church, its people, and its mission to the community and the world is not seen by anyone, there will be no reason for anyone to want to join. UU churches have a unique and important message for the world that, among other things, is about sharing compassion, acceptance, and dignity for all people across all religious traditions. We do not require adherence to one creed as a precondition to acceptance and inclusion. We do not insist that there is only one truth or one way to seek truth. That is the great strength and the hidden gem of Unitarian Universalism. The world is naturally a beautiful blend of diversity not homogeneity and the culture and religion of the future must reflect rather than deny this truth. If, however, we keep this UU gem of universal compassion and acceptance hidden from view, it will not be embraced by future generations.

Let your light shine!

UU churches do great work in social justice, community enrichment, and spiritual development for people of all faiths. If we let people know about what we are doing then those who resonate with our cause will want to know more. Every time the church does anything its name and mission should be made visible and clear. At every opportunity let people know who you are, what you do, and why you do it because there are others who want to be part of your good work. There are people out there who are passionate about what the UU movement stands for–they just don't know about it yet. Give them every opportunity to find out. Reach out to every community of every person and let them know about you. That presence can be on many fronts including live events, recorded activities, and through an online or social media presence. Cultivating relationships with other organizations, people, and sites with similar goals helps to create a greater web of relationship and interaction.

Conclusion

The goal of Radical Hospitality is at the heart of what Unitarian Universalism is about but it is not easy. Systemic racism and oppression is difficult to dismantle and overcome precisely because it is embedded into long standing systems. Old habits and processes can be comforting and regenerative to those who habituate them and because they are fixed in time they are less likely to be examined in the light of changing realities.

The thing about oppressive systems is that they can unconsciously be maintained by very well meaning individuals. People who genuinely strive to be anti-racist or anti-oppressive may perpetuate the exclusionary practices of their institution simply through repetition To say that something should be done because it is how it's always been done may preserve oppressive practices.

Our congregations can reflect the beautiful multi-diverse range of human abilities, cultures, philosophies, and expressions in a way that embraces peace, cooperation, and mutual support. UU churches can be the hope of the future but it will take great passion, work, and dedication to that dream to make it a reality.

Like an artful masterpiece, Radical Hospitality requires a grand vision and the application of a great deal of time and effort to manifest that vision. Great paintings require patience and the commitment to a dream so that it can take form and shape over time.

The work of Radical Hospitality will need a dream to keep

it anchored. Those who work on it will need to be patient with themselves and with each other. Change incurs fear and fear incurs resistance and defensiveness. Compassion is needed for the long-term church member as well as for the newcomer. Renewal is not an either/or proposal. It can be more of an also/and way of working together.

The work of Radical Hospitality is ultimately sacred work. It is done not for individual advancement but for the betterment of the church, its people, and its community. It is holy work toward building wholeness. It is the work of opening up to more compassion and empathy starting from the self and expanding outward to the community and then outward further to those not yet known. Such expansiveness makes room for more love and more love creates room for more joy. Radical Hospitality, simply put, is the act of loving to love.

Appendices

Scriptures About Welcoming

<u>Judaism</u>

You shall not oppress a resident alien; you know the heart of an alien, for you were aliens in the land of Egypt.
    ~ Exodus 23:9

When an alien resides with you in your land, you shall not oppress the alien. The alien who resides with you shall be to you as the citizen among you; you shall love the alien as yourself, for you were aliens in the land of Egypt: I am the Lord your God.
    ~Leviticus 19:33-34

<u>Christianity</u>

For I was hungry and you gave me food, I was thirsty and you gave me something to drink, I was a stranger and you welcomed me, I was naked and you gave me clothing, I was sick and you took care of me, I was in prison and you visited me. Then the righteous will answer him, 'Lord, when was it that we saw you hungry and gave you food, or thirsty and gave you something to drink? And when was it that we saw you as a stranger and welcomed you, or naked and gave you clothing? And when was it that we saw you sick or in prison and visited you?' And the king will answer them, 'Truly I tell you, just as you did it to one of the least of these who are members of my family, you did it to me.
    ~Mathew 25:35-40

Let mutual love continue. Do not neglect to show hospitality to strangers, for by doing that some have entertained angels without knowing it.
~Hebrew 13:1-2

Islam

Worship Allah, and ascribe no partners to Him, and be good to the parents, and the relatives, and the orphans, and the poor, and the neighbor next door, and the distant neighbor, and the close associate, and the traveler, and your servants. Allah does not love the arrogant showoff.
~Surah 4:36

They ask you what they should give. Say, "Whatever charity you give is for the parents, and the relatives, and the orphans, and the poor, and the wayfarer. Whatever good you do, Allah is aware of it.
~Surah 2:215

Buddhism

Cultivate an all-embracing mind of love
For all throughout the universe,
In all its height, depth and breadth.
~The Metta Sutta: 8

Confucian

When a guest [from afar] could not find a place to stay, Confucius would say to him, I have a place for you in my house. [In fact, you are welcome here] when you are living, and should you die while you are staying with me, I can also arrange to have your funeral in my house.
~The Rites

Hindu

Let a person never turn away a stranger from his house, that is the rule. Therefore a man should, by all means, acquire much food, for good people say to the stranger: 'There is enough food for you.
~Taitiriya Upanishad 1.11.2

Sikh

None is our enemy, none is stranger to us, we are in accord with one and all.
~Guru Granth Sahib

Baha'i

One amongst His Teachings is this, that love and good faith must so dominate the human heart that men will regard the stranger as a familiar friend, the malefactor as one of their own, the alien even as a loved one, the enemy as a companion dear and close.
~The Writings of Abdu'l-Baha

Taoism

Become one with Dao, and Dao welcomes you. Become one with De, and De welcomes you. Become one with loss, and loss welcomes you. If you aren't worthy of trust, others won't trust you.
~Tao Te Ching, Verse 23

The UU Principles and their Relationship to Radical Hospitality

Principle 1: *The inherent worth and dignity of every person.*
  • Perhaps the best known of all the principles, Principle One admonishes UUs to treat each other, whether stranger or not, with equal worth and dignity.

Principle 2: *Justice, equity and compassion in human relations.*
  • Principle Two is focused specifically on human

relationships and adds to the first principle the need to treat everyone with compassion.

Principle 3: *Acceptance of one another and encouragement to spiritual growth in our congregations.*
  • The third principle begins with a call to accept each other unconditionally. Welcoming is a form of open acceptance.

Principle 6. *The goal of world community with peace, liberty, and justice for all.*
  • The Sixth Principle describes a realized vision of a world where all people welcome and relate to each other as neighbors.

Principle 7. *Respect for the interdependent web of all existence of which we are a part.*
  • The image of a world community of peace in the sixth principle is expanded into a vision of an interconnected web of existence between all beings.

Proposed Principle 8. *Journeying toward spiritual wholeness by working to build a diverse multicultural Beloved Community by our actions that accountably dismantle racism and other oppressions in ourselves and our institutions.*
  • Perhaps the most significant principle concerning welcoming and its relationship to the reduction of the oppression of marginalized communities is expressed in the proposed Eighth Principle. Though not currently an official part of the UU principles, many congregations have voted to adopt it and its popularity is gaining ground throughout the country. Its emphasis is on the importance of diversity and multiculturalism which are some of the results of a successful radical hospitality program.

The Visioning Process

Questions to ask:

1. Why do you want to take on the work of radical hospitality?

2. What does your local community look like?
    1. (check local census data)

3. What people in your community are marginalized?

4. What people in your church are marginalized?

5. What does your congregation think about diversity?
    1. (administer a Diversity Survey)
    2. What work needs to be done?

6. What work has your church already done toward essential invitation?
    1. (administer a Site Review)
    2. What work needs to be done?

7. What work has your church already done toward radical welcoming?
    1. (administer a Worship Service Review)
    2. What work needs to be done?

8. What local organizations could you reach out toward to help with this work?

9. Is your church ready to fully embrace other people unconditionally?
    1. What things can be done to demonstrate that commitment to others?

10. Are you and your church willing to learn more and discuss:
    1. Cultural competence?
    2. Radical welcoming?

3. Anti-racism?
4. Patterns of systemic power?

11. Is your church prepared to deal with the fear and uncertainty that is endemic to this work?

Diversity Survey

To be distributed to the congregation and staff.

1. How would you describe the diversity in the church?

2. Have you ever felt marginalized in the church?
   Please share your experience.

3. Have others been marginalized in the church?
   Please share your experience.

4. Do you feel the church values all cultures, identities, abilities, and backgrounds?
   If not, why?

5. Does the church live out its values through the actions of its members?
   If not, why?

6. Do you feel welcome and accepted in church services and activities?
   If not, why?

7. Are others welcomed and accepted in church services and activities?
   If not, why?

8. Are newcomers welcomed and accepted in church services and activities?
   If not, why?

Site Review

The website:
- Easy to navigate
- Attractive and inviting
    - Includes photos of activities
- Includes information important to visitors on home page
    - Worship times
    - Address and directions
    - Contact information
    - Safety information
- Includes pages specifically designed for visitors
    - What to expect when visiting
    - Service times
    - Accessibility
    - Safety protocols
    - Directions to the church
    - Photo of front entrance
    - Parking directions and information
    - FAQ - frequently asked questions

The parking lot:
- Guest parking available
- Handicapped parking available
- Overflow parking available

The church:
- Well lit
- Clean
- Free from odors
- Safe

Signage to and from:
- Bathrooms
- Fellowship hall
- Sanctuary
- Entrance

- Parking lot
  - Visitors
  - Handicapped
  - Overflow

Front entrance:
- A sign
- Temporary name tags
- Directions to the Information Center
- A building map

Art spaces
- presentations of art by traditionally marginalized people
  - Visual art
  - Written forms
  - Performances

The Information Center
- Located near the entrance (if possible)
- Accessible and noticeable
- Filled with information (separate or together)
  - About the church
  - About Unitarian Universalism
  - Contact cards
    - Include Ambassador Program
  - How to become a member
  - A list of committees and groups
  - How to become active in groups and events
  - Building Map
- Equipped with pencils
- Equipped with temporary name tags (if not at the entrance)
  - Information about what different name tags represent
  - Application for permanent name tags

Members Area
- Permanent (member) name tags
- Provide names of committee members

- Bulletin board

Sanctuary
- Clean
- Well lit
- Good sound
- Display screen
- Symbolism

Worship Service Review

Parking
- Is it easy to find parking?
- Is it easy to find the church entrance?

Building
- Is it safe?
- Is it comfortable?
- Is it easy for someone to find their way around?
- Can people find or access information?
  - About the church?
  - About Unitarian Universalism?

Greeters
- Where are they?
- Are they easily identifiable?
- Are they helpful?
- What do they do?

Ushers
- Where are they?
- Are they easily identifiable?
- Are they helpful?
- What do they do?

Order of Service
- Is it clear?
- Is it cluttered?
- Is it easy to follow?
- Is it useful for a visitor?
- Does it include enough information?

- Does it include contact and follow-up information?

Service

- Are newcomers welcomed?
- Is the service inviting and engaging for visitors?

After service

- Are newcomers contacted after the service?
- How are they contacted?
- When are they contacted?
- Is the contact effective?

Secret Guest Instructions

Thank you for volunteering to review our church. Your input will help us to become more open and welcoming to anyone who may come to visit us.

The goal of your visit is to blend in as much as a newcomer can. Introduce yourself as an interested visitor but do not tell them you are doing a review of the church. As you enter the building and join in the activities of worship and socialization, pay careful attention to everything a new person might want to know and experience. If you need to take notes try not to be conspicuous about it. Take a look at the Secret Guest questions before you go so that you have an idea of what to examine and, of course, feel free to add any additional comments or suggestions. At the end of your visit please submit a report to the person who asked you to do this service.

Secret Guest Questions

1. Were you able to find your way to the church?

2. If you drove, were you able to find parking?

3. If you did not drive, were you able to find transportation to the church?

4. Were you able to find your way into the church?

5. Did the church feel safe and comfortable?

6. Were you able to find your way to the sanctuary or worship space?

7. Were you able to access information about the church?

8. Were there greeters and were they helpful?

9. Were there ushers and were they helpful?

10. Was the worship experience positive and inspiring?

11. Did you feel welcomed throughout your visit

12. Would you be inclined to return?

Further Reading

Gentile, Yvonne and Debi Nixon. *The Art Of Hospitality: A Practical Guide for a Ministry of Radical Welcome*. Nashville: Abingdon Press, 2020.

Kaur, Valarie. *See No Stranger: A Memoir and Manifesto of Revolutionary Love*. One World, 2020.

Kearney, Richard, and Melissa Fitzpatrick. *Radical Hospitality : From Thought to Action*. First edition., First ed., Fordham University Press, 2021.

Malm, Jonathan. *Unwelcome: 50 Ways Churches Drive Away First-Time Visitors*. Los Angeles: The Center For Church Communication, 2014.

Nixon, Debi and Yvonne Gentile. *The Art Of Hospitality: A Practical Guide for a Ministry of Radical Welcome*. Nashville: Abingdon Press, 2020.

Nelson, Linnea. *Beyond Welcome: Building Communities of Love.* Boston: Skinner House Books, 2021.

Rainer, Thom. *Becoming A Welcoming Church.* Nashville, TN: B&H Publishing Group, 2018.

Robertson, Brandan. *True Inclusion: Creating Communities of Radical Embrace.* St. Louis: Chalice Press, 2018.

Spellers, Stephanie. *Radical Welcome: Embracing God, the Other, and the Spirit of Transformation.* New York: Church Publishing, 2006.

About The Author

Kenneth P. Langer

Rev. Dr. Kenneth P. Langer is an ordained Universalist minister and a former college professor with graduate degrees in both music and theology. He is a published writer, composer, and poet and is the author of several works of fiction as well as books on spiritual living. He also enjoys playing and designing games.

Learn more by visiting his website: http://kennethplanger.com

He also enjoys playing and designing games.

Learn more by visiting his website: http://kennethplanger.com

Other Books

Non-Fiction

- Spirituality
  - A Different Calling: A Manual for Lay Ministers and Other Non-Professional Facilitators of Any Spiritual Tradition
  - Many Leaves, One Tree: A Collection of Aphorisms Inspired by the Tao Te Ching
  - The Purpose Derived Life: What In The Universe Am I Here For?
  - Three Guidelines for Ethical Living
  - Playing Cards and the Game of Living Well
  - The Emergence of God: The Intersection of Science, Nature, and Spirituality
  - The Langer Deck
  - Emergent Spirituality: Principles and Practices at the Intersection of Science, Nature, and Spirituality
  - Open Hearts and Open Doors: Radical Hospitality in the Church
  - Let Us Wander: A Ministry of Music and Arts
  - Pastoral Reflections: A Collection of Sermons, Book One
- Games
  - 52 New Card Games (For Those Old Cards)
  - 36 New Dice Games
  - 40 Games for Forty Dice
  - Castle Imbroglio: An Escape Adventure Book
- Music

- A Guide to the Art of Musical Performance
- A Theory for All Music
  - Book 1: Fundamentals
  - Book 2: Chords and Part-Writing
  - Book 3: The Tools of Analysis
  - Book 4: Parametric Analysis
- Rounds and Canons for Peace and Justice
- Music for Unitarian-Universalist Choirs
- Songs of Worship
- 50 Songs for Meditation

Fiction

- Science Fiction
  - The Milleran Cluster Series
    - Of Eternal Light
    - The Forever Horizon
    - The Suicide Fire
    - The Song of the Mother
    - The Journey of Awri
- Theater
  - Four Comedies
  - 10 x 10: Ten Ten-Minute Plays Book 1
  - 10 x 10: Ten Ten-Minute Plays Book 2
  - 10 x 10: Ten Ten-Minute Plays Book 3
  - 10 x 10:Ten Ten-Minute Plays Book 4
  - Ageless Wisdom: Multigenerational Plays for Worship
- Poetry
  - Looking At The World: A Collection of Poetry
  - Prayers

Final Note

Thank you for reading this book!

If you enjoyed reading it please let me know
and please consider writing a positive online review.

Ken Langer

Contact Information
personal website: http://kennethplanger.com
book site: http://brassbellbooks.com
Email: revklanger@gmail.com

www.ingramcontent.com/pod-product-compliance
Lightning Source LLC
La Vergne TN
LVHW041206080426
835508LV00008B/828